sporadic

avary gray

Presentation by *BookLeaf Publishing*

Web: www.bookleafpub.com

E-mail: info@bookleafpub.com

ISBN: 9789358312515

First edition 2023

this book is dedicated to my little sister. i love you beyond measure and i hope as you grow you understand everything i am going through. the day the time comes please run to me so we can go through this together.

ACKNOWLEDGEMENT

thank you to my family and friends for standing by me through everything. thank you to whoever is reading this for taking the time to hear me, and understand me.

on the brink of battle

my brain is drawing continuous circles, so often
and repeatedly you'd think they'd have a
purpose.
when i choose to sporadically think
NOTHING...
my brain goes into overdrive to overthink
SOMETHING...
do i do this or that? this or that?
decisions seem to make me crazy even though i
want to say they don't phase me.
as my brain chooses again to ponder
i am about to fight a dangerous monster
on the brink of battle...
but i will not be rattled...

flowers

don't pot me if you do not intend for me to grow.

please do not over or under water me, then offer
me your sorrow.

if that is the case, please leave me in peace
where the sun will help me glow.

i have been so malnourished i might never get
the chance to flourish.

please do not blame me when my leaves wilt.

you have trimmed all the good parts and left me
with nothing but self guilt.

free

please don't go.

please don't leave me here alone.

you have not shown me how to live and survive
on my own.

i begged and pleaded on my hands and knees.

you have to take me with you, please!

as you told me you love me,

you have never looked so free.

today marks the day i'll start to grieve.

today marks the day you had to leave.

grandma i am begging, please don't go.

there is still so much in this world that i don't
know.

i don't know how to grow.

one more time, please don't go.

i feel broke.

word 1

obscure, even though you didn't ask, my favorite word is obscure.

not the good kind of obscure when you wonder when God will bless you next, or the obscure feeling when you're going to get a raise or get promoted, but for sure one of things will happen, obscure.

the type of obscure when it's just you in a pitch black room with your thoughts alone, or so you think, obscure.

the type of obscure i would use to describe a broken person with a beautiful word and a negative connotation, obscure.

obscure meaning uncertain, could be adequately used to describe my emotions, obscure.

it is such a powerful word somehow it seems to hold the reality of my recent decisions and thoughts, obscure.

do not feel obscure, this word comes with a
burden. so heavy it could make you feel obscure
about your whole life, obscure.

the type of obscure i am feeling is unsafe,
obscure.

obscure emotions hold an obscure reality.

obscure...

self

you held me so tightly why?
you talked to me so softly but why?
you kissed me so gently but why?
you spent so much time with me but why?
you cared so much for me but why?
you loved my so compassionately but why?

i did nothing but reciprocate.
i held you tightly.
i talked to you softly.
i kissed you gently.
i spent so much time with you.
i loved you compassionately.
but you left me, why?

what did she do that i didn't?
what did she do that i couldn't?
what does she have that i don't?

sometimes i think i could've been more, i
could've done more, but it wasn't about me. it
was never anything i did wrong. i am simply me.
i love what you lost. i am now more than ever.
love lost as some would say, but love gained is
how i feel.

self love, self worth, and self respect.
this was never about me this was about you, but
it is now more than ever, me.

all me.

nothing but me.

company

i enjoy my company.
i enjoy my company when my company doesn't
over stay their welcome.
my company only visits me when i am asleep.
my company isn't pleasant.
my company visits from midnight until i make
my company leave, when i am able to wake up.
my company doesn't have a distinct face but has
distinct figures.
my company never comes alone, they visit in
groups.
strange shadows that stand over me while i
sleep.
my company never speaks, and my company
never seems to leave, let alone sleep.
my company never fails to make an appearance.
my company has become inherent.

superman

to my hero, thank you for being my mother and
my father on the days my mother was absent.

thank you for teaching me the girly things my
mother should have taught me, and treating me
like a son to make me strong.

thank you for always turning up at my most
important events, and being a shoulder to cry on.

i am sorry when you call i don't always answer,
and sometimes you feel forgotten.

i am sorry if sometimes you feel unappreciated
or unloved.

between you and i, you are forever and always
my favorite, my hero.

to my dad, you are my inspiration.
to my father, you make me so proud everyday.
to my hero, to say i love you is an
understatement.
to the most important person in my life, thank
you for being you.

unfinished

i don't have many words to describe this, other
than friendship gone wrong.
but if you ask me it kinda played like a never
ending song.

i loved and cared for you with everything in me,
but nothing came from you except envy.

i don't really know why you became friends with
me in the first place,
all you do is get mad and say you need space.

i wanted to finish this poem because there was
so much i had to say but i am now realizing
writing about you isn't worth my time.

analogies to describe my apologies for my mental state

while driving things appeared smaller, because i
was watching though my rearview. we crashed
because i didn't have a clear view.
this wasn't about my car...

a monster lives under my bed. he grows larger
each time you feed him. i try to calm down and
think best case scenario before he gets fed.
this isn't about a monster...

every time you spend a dollar a little part of your
net worth is gone. you are broke. until you
remember your budget can be redrawn.
this isn't about finances.

i saw what seemed to be a sand pit. i love sand.
as i jumped in like a kid on christmas, this sand
pit consumed everything i had in hand. i didn't
understand all of this was just so unplanned.
this wasn't about a sand pit...

i had a dream. i started a new job. i was in a
meeting, unable to speak. everyone conversing

around me. dressed in my pajamas. it belittled
my self esteem.
this wasn't about a dream...

love is

who is love?

i cannot describe who love is in one word.
matter fact, i can only describe love by who i
thought he was.

love is not patient, love is not kind.

love doesn't understand how to communicate.

love gets angry, and lashes out sometimes.

love plays victim a lot, and then doesn't know
why i'm upset.

love is in pain, a terrible actress trying to hide
emotions.

love has a lot of potential but doesn't know how
to apply it.

love is a cheater.

now, i thought love was gentle, caring and
genuine. i thought love wanted every part of me,

including the bad. i thought love knew how to
love me. i thought love knew what to do with
my emotions and how to handle me when i
broke down.

it turns out my perception of love was wrong. i
know the real love, all of the bad and ugly parts
of love.

but i want a different love.

i want love to care, and to be genuine. i want
love to be kind and gentle with my emotions, to
understand how to communicate.

but most importantly, i want love to understand
how to love.

until then, goodbye to love for now.

from my ex

"i want you, i miss you, i think of you, i dream
of you, i adore you, i need you... you name tastes
sweet leaving the tip of my tongue. as i speak
into existence and proclaim that you are mine.
you're more than a beautiful smile, i see world's
hidden behind your eyes, worlds of possibilities.
the possibility of being happy with our mini
we's. i'd die for you, yes physically.
but what i really mean is that i'd kill the man i
am to become all you really need.
a phoenix from the ashes, i'll give birth to love
and let is breath.
there's forests in your heart, no i'm not talking
trees.
the love you have has brough fruit to my life,
while all i grew was weeds.
it's thanks to you i've cleared some land and
started planting seeds,
to be a better man, an honest man, and show a
realer me.
know that you're enough and you are realer than
i've tend to be,
yes i have been rough, but i've learned how to
love with gentle ease.

my mind runs amok but it's with you my heart
can be at peace.
at night when you're asleep, i ask the Lord that
he will keep you.
I haven't been honest, now i'm trying to be see
through, cure the darkness in heart, and hope
that i can keep you.
yes i can be happy, but what's happy when i need
you, but what others when i see you." from my
ex.

what is

when i think of the word mother it gives me a
bad taste in my mouth.
i don't understand what a mother is, just how i
know i have to be.
if i had to say anything to my mother it would be
i love you.

i love you even though you have taught me the
difference a mom and a mother.

i love you even though i have never been enough
for you.

you have never held me equal to my other
siblings, you have never held me or cared for me
the same.

i have always gotten the rougher version of you.

now i search for a gentle compassionate
character every time i meet an older woman.

i feel the need to be cared for. i crave a mother.
the nurturing aspects i never seemed to receive.
the texts and phone calls when we're both busy.

the things you were supposed to teach me, that
as a 20 year-old i still don't know how to do to
this day.

i love you but where are you.
i love you but where have you been.
i love you, and when you're ready to learn how
to be my mother i will be waiting with open
arms.

you are hurt. i see you. i hear you. i understand
you. but please don't hold it against me, the way
your relationship ended had nothing to do with
me, none of your pas of future was my fault.
please do not hold me accountable. i love you.

i will love you until you won't allow me to love
you anymore.

to the Marine Corps

wow where do i start.

this one goes out to the corps, for always giving
me a sense of purpose.
for allowing me to fit in where i can and have a
stable job.
for providing me benefits.
for giving me free therapy.
for paying for my food and housing.
for giving me friends like no other.

but one thing that i cannot thank you for is
hating on me because i am a woman.

letting men talk to me or treat me differently
because i have different hair or uniform
regulations.

for sweeping my sexual assault under the rug
after i came to you and told you i was hurting
and embarrassed.

for giving me the option to request mast when i
am being treated unfairly, then asking what you
can do to avoid me requesting it all together.

for calling me crazy when i am sad and request
to go to behavioral health to get treatment even
though i am more courageous than the man next
to me that won't admit he needs help.

for calling me a bitch when i stick up for myself
because if not me than who.

to the Marine Corps...
you could've done more...

growth

i never understood why people pull weeds.
weeds grow significantly faster than normal
plants.
if people grew like weeds the potential of the
normal population would grow at unnormal
speeds.
people are so quick to pull them they don't
deeply think about their true enchant.
i want to grow like a weed.
i can then sprinkle the seeds.
which will allow me to succeed.

anxious

anxiety is like a disease.
i cannot seem like to get rid of it.
it follows me everywhere, like a dog on a leash.
my thoughts are the worst, causing me not to go
places i would normally go.
making me sit in the house, trying to find the
courage to leave.
making me think differently about myself even
though i know who i am.
anxiety has this weird way of just going in
circles.
i push it out and it finds a way to walk right back
in.

another one

i love you here.
i love you there.
i love you every where.
i love you the same.
i love you differently.
i love you to in the morning.
i love you at night.
i love you at all times when it's bright.
i love you and all aspects of you.
to me, i love me.

step-mom

what is the difference between a step mom, and
a mother?

i couldn't tell you.
i have seen so many movies where there is
always a scary step mom,
but not mine
she was God's gift to me because i needed a
mother.
i needed to learn how to be a woman before i
grew up.
i still need her when i go to the store.
i still need her when i go to the doctor.
i still need her when i receive amazing news.
my step mother is mother, and simply that.
the most caring woman i have met.
she has never turned her back on me. I cannot
thank her enough.

future me

to future me.
you are amazing, please do not forget that no
matter where you are going, and what you
become i will always be proud of you.

do not forget the woman you are, and the woman
you are raising.

do not forget about the mistakes i have made
when you carry on with out me.

please do not look back i will not be lonely just
keep moving forward.

please stop being too nice not everyone deserves
all of you, the best parts.

stay motivated, and love all that you do.